MULES
&
EARLY POEMS

Also by Paul Muldoon:

WHY BROWNLEE LEFT
QUOOF

Paul Muldoon

Mules & Early Poems

[signed] Paul Muldoon

[inscription] Richmond November 87

Wake Forest University Press

Published by Wake Forest University Press,
Winston-Salem, N.C. 27109

ACKNOWLEDGEMENTS

Mules was first published in 1977 by Wake Forest University Press and Faber and Faber; *Early Poems* were selected from *New Weather* published by Faber and Faber in 1973. "Wind and Tree" has been revised.

CONTENTS

EARLY POEMS

EARLY POEMS

WIND AND TREE

In the way that the most of the wind
Happens where there are trees,

Most of the world is centred
About ourselves.

Often where the wind has gathered
The trees together,

One tree will take
Another in her arms and hold.

Their branches that are grinding
Madly together,

It is no real fire.
They are breaking each other.

Often I think I should be like
The single tree, going nowhere,

Since my own arm could not and would not
Break the other. Yet by my broken bones

I tell new weather.

THRUSH

I guessed the letter
    Must be yours. I recognised
The cuttle ink,
    The serif on
The P. I read the postmark and the date
    Impatience held
By a paperweight.
    I took your letter at eleven
To the garden
    With my tea.
And suddenly the yellow gum secreted
    Halfwayup
The damson bush
    Had grown a shell.
I let those scentless pages fall
    And took it
In my feckless hand. I turned it over
    On its back
To watch your mouth
    Withdraw. Making a lean, white fist
Out of my freckled hand.

THE GLAD EYE

Bored by Ascham and Zeno
In private conversation on the longbow,

I went out onto the lawn.
Taking the crooked bow of yellow cane,

I shot an arrow over
The house and wounded my brother.

He cried those huge dark tears
Till they had blackened half his hair.

Zeno could have had no real
Notion of the flying arrow being still,

Not blessed with the hindsight
Of photography and the suddenly frozen shot,

Yet that obstinate one
Eye inveigled me to a standing stone.

Evil eyes have always burned
Corn black and people have never churned

Again after their blink.
That eye was deeper than the Lake of the Young,

Outstared the sun in the sky.
Could look without commitment into another eye.

DANCERS AT THE MOY

This Italian square
And circling plain
Black once with mares
And their stallions,
The flat Blackwater
Turning its stones

Over hour after hour
As their hooves shone
And lifted together
Under the black rain,
One or other Greek war
Now coloured the town

Blacker than ever before
With hungry stallions
And their hungry mares
Like hammocks of skin,
The flat Blackwater
Unable to contain

Itself as horses poured
Over acres of grain
In a black and gold river.
No band of Athenians
Arrived at the Moy fair
To buy for their campaign,

16

Peace having been declared
And a treaty signed.
The black and gold river
Ended as a trickle of brown
Where those horses tore
At briars and whins,

Ate the flesh of each other
Like people in famine.
The flat Blackwater
Hobbled on its stones
With a wild stagger
And sag in its backbone,

The local people gathered
Up the white skeletons.
Horses buried for years
Under the foundations
Give their earthen floors
The ease of trampolines.

17

THE WAKING FATHER

My father and I are catching spricklies
Out of the Oona river.
They have us feeling righteous,
The way we have thrown them back.
Our benevolence is astounding.

When my father stood out in the shallows
It occurred to me that
The spricklies might have been piranhas,
The river a red carpet
Rolling out from where he had just stood,

Or I wonder now if he is dead or sleeping.
For if he is dead I would have his grave
Secret and safe,
I would turn the river out of its course,
Lay him in its bed, bring it round again.

              No one would question
That he had treasures or his being a king,
Telling now of the real fish farther down.

IDENTITIES

When I reached the sea
I fell in with another who had just come
From the interior. Her family
Had figured in a past regime
But her father was now imprisoned.

She had travelled, only by night,
Escaping just as her own warrant
Arrived and stealing the police boat,
As far as this determined coast.

As it happened, we were staying at the same
Hotel, pink and goodish for the tourist
Quarter. She came that evening to my room
Asking me to go to the capital,
Offering me wristwatch and wallet,
To search out an old friend who would steal
Papers for herself and me. Then to be married,
We could leave from that very harbour.

I have been wandering since, back up the streams
That had once flowed simply one into the other,
One taking the other's name.

CLONFEACLE

It happened not far away
In this meadowland
That Patrick lost a tooth.
I translate the placename

As we walk along
The river where he washed,
That translates stone to silt.
The river would preach

As well as Patrick did.
A tongue of water passing
Between teeth of stones.
Making itself clear,

Living by what it says,
Converting meadowland to marsh.
You turn towards me,
Coming round to my way

Of thinking, holding
Your tongue between your teeth.
I turn my back on the river
And Patrick, their sermons

Ending in the air.

FEBRUARY

He heard that in Derryscollop there is a tree
For every day of the year,
And the extra tree is believed to grow
One year in every four.

He had never yet taken time to grieve
For this one without breasts
Or that one wearing her heart on her sleeve
Or another with her belly slashed.

He had never yet taken time to love
The blind pink fledgeling fallen out of the nest
Of one sleeping with open mouth
And her head at a list.

What was he watching and waiting for,
Walking Scollop every day?
For one intending to leave at the end of the year,
Who would break the laws of time and stay.

KATE WHISKEY

I kept the whiskey in the caves
Well up in the hills. It was never safe
To have it about the houses,
Always crawling with excise and police.

The people could still get the stuff
As often as they liked, and easily enough,
For those were still the days
When making whiskey broke nobody's laws.

Selling it, though, was as grave
An offence as teaching those people to love,
Fathers and husbands and boys.

Water rushed through my caves with a noise
To tell me how I should always live.
I sold the water, the whiskey I would give.

VESPERS

It looks like there's
Nothing for it
But the bare floor.
You've given one blanket
Off the single bed

By way of reasonableness.
Couldn't we go to sleep
Together for once,
If only of necessity?
We could always keep

The sheet between us.
I'll do nothing you won't.
We'll both be colder
For being lost in thought,
Setting up difficulties

Where none ought to exist.
I'll put out the light,
And the night has fallen
Bodily and silent
Through the defunct window.

The frost has designs on it.

THE CURE FOR WARTS

Had I been the seventh son of a seventh son
Living at the dead centre of a wood
Or at the dead end of a lane,
I might have cured by my touch alone
That pair of warts nippling your throat,

Who had no faith in a snail rubbed on your skin
And spiked on a thorn like a king's head,
In my spittle on shrunken stone,
In bathing yourself at the break of dawn
In dew or the black cock's or the bull's blood,

In other such secrets told by way of a sign
Of the existence of one or other god,
So I doubt if any woman's son
Could have cured by his touch alone
That pair of warts nibbling your throat.

LEAVING AN ISLAND

The woman of the house
Is letting out the chickens.
Air trapped in the capsized

Boat where they coop
Is visible to the naked eye.
I see through you

In your crocheted dress.
Elevenses. Woman of the house,
This is just to say

We have left no clues.
Ferdinand, Miranda,
It was pure and simple.

Thank you, thank you.
For the dulse. For everything.
I read between your legs

And recognise that you who took
The world into your mouth
Have taught me ships in bottles,

The sea in shells.

GOOD FRIDAY, 1971. DRIVING WESTWARD

It was good going along with the sun
Through Ballygawley, Omagh and Strabane.
I started out as it was getting light
And caught sight of hares all along the road
That looked to have been taking a last fling,
Doves making the most of their offerings
As if all might not be right with the day

Where I moved through morning towards the sea.
I was glad that I would not be alone.
Those children who travel badly as wine
Waved as they passed in their uppity cars
And now the first cows were leaving the byres,
The first lorry had delivered its load.
A whole country was fresh after the night

Though people were still fighting for the last
Dreams and changing their faces where I paused
To read the first edition of the truth.
I gave a lift to the girl out of love
And crossed the last great frontier at Lifford.
Marooned by an iffing and butting herd
Of sheep, Letterkenny had just then laid

Open its heart and we passed as new blood
Back into the grey flesh of Donegal.
The sky went out of its way for the hills
And life was changing down for the sharp bends
Where the road had put its thin brown arm round
A hill and held on tight out of pure fear.
Errigal stepped out suddenly in our

Path and the thin arm tightened round the waist
Of the mountain and for a time I lost
Control and she thought we hit something big
But I had seen nothing, perhaps a stick
Lying across the road. I glanced back once
And there was nothing but a heap of stones.
We had just dropped in from nowhere for lunch

In Gaoth Dobhair, I happy and she convinced
Of the death of more than lamb or herring.
She stood up there and then, face full of drink,
And announced that she and I were to blame
For something killed along the way we came.
Children were warned that it was rude to stare,
Left with their parents for a breath of air.

SEANCHAS

Coming here, we were like that mountain whose base
We kept sidestepping. Thinking ourselves superior.
Having, we thought, our final attitude and bias.
Really, wanting a new slant. For the past hour
We heard the seanchai relearn
What he has always known,

Region of heroes, gentle maidens,
Giants that war and landgrab.
Each phrase opening like a fern.
Till some make fists of themselves, like the stones
In a landslide, a cadence
That comes in his way. He can adlib
No other route. If we play back the tape
He may take up where he left off.

Nothing. And no heroes people this landscape
Through which he sees us off.
The lifted wondering faces of his sheep
Stare back at us like nimble rain clouds, their bellies
Accumulate and, are anonymous again. But having shape,
Separate and memorable.

HEDGEHOG

The snail moves like a
Hovercraft, held up by a
Rubber cushion of itself,
Sharing its secret

With the hedgehog. The hedgehog
Shares its secret with no one.
We say, Hedgehog, come out
Of yourself and we will love you.

We mean no harm. We want
Only to listen to what
You have to say. We want
Your answers to our questions.

The hedgehog gives nothing
Away, keeping itself to itself.
We wonder what a hedgehog
Has to hide, why it so distrusts.

We forget the god
Under this crown of thorns.
We forget that never again
Will a god trust in the world.

LIVES OF THE SAINTS

Others have sought publicity
But the saints looked for higher things.
The people getting ready to fly
Off the rooves of public buildings
Had their eyes on the actual sky,
Never spreading their linen or bamboo wings

So briefly for a public death
Had they really been saints of the old school.
Those saints have the last laugh
At the reporters for the Chronicles
And the people taking photographs.
I think especially of Brendan setting sail

One day the sea was blueblack
As his body that overnight he had beaten,
Drifting along wherever God liked
And the people living by bread alone
Shouting after Good Luck, Good Luck.
All the Chronicles agreed. The boat was stone.

THE INDIANS ON ALCATRAZ

Through time their sharp features
Have softened and blurred,
As if they still inhabited
The middle distances,
As if these people have never
Stopped riding hard

In an opposite direction,
The people of the shattered lances
Who have seemed forever going back.
To have willed this reservation,
It is as if they are decided
To be islanders at heart,

As if this island
Has forever been the destination
Of all those dwindling bands.
After the newspaper and T.V. reports
I want to be glad that
Young Man Afraid Of His Horses Lives

As a brilliant guerrilla fighter,
The weight of his torque
Worn like the moon's last quarter,
Though only if he believes
As I believed of his fathers,
That they would not attack after dark.

ELIZABETH

The birds begin as an isolated shower
Over the next county, their slow waltz
Swerving as if to avoid something
Every so often, getting thin
As it slants, making straight for
Us over your father's darkening fields,
Till their barely visible wings
Remember themselves, they are climbing again.
We wonder what could bring them this far

Inland, they belong to the sea.
You hold on hard like holding on to life,
Following the flock as it bends
And collapses like a breeze.
You want to know where from and why,
But birds would never keep still long enough
For me to be able to take a count.
We'll hold our ground and they'll pass.
But they're coming right overhead, you cry,

And storm inside and bang the door.
All I can hear is the flicking of bolts.
The one dull window is shutting
Its eye as if a wayward hurricane
With the name of a girl and the roar
Of devils were beginning its assaults.
But these are the birds of a child's painting,
Filling the page till nothing else is seen.
You are inside yet, pacing the floor,

Having been trapped in every way.
You hold yourself as your own captive,
My promised children are in your hands,
Hostaged by you in your father's old house.
I call you now for all the names of the day,
Lizzie and Liz and plain Beth.
You do not make the slightest sound.
When you decide that you have nothing to lose
And come out, there is nothing you can say,

We watch them hurtle, a recklessness of stars,
Into the acre that has not cooled
From my daylong ploughings and harrowings,
Their greys flecking the brown,
Till one, and then two, and now four
Sway back across your father's patchwork quilt,
Into your favourite elm. They will stay long
Enough to underline how soon they will be gone,
As you seem thinner than you were before.

THE LOST TRIBE

Has it been only two years
Since the river went on fire?
Last year your father's heart wob-
Bled while he was dusting crops,

Too heavy for his light plane.
Was it three years ago, then,
The year I shot the wild duck
And we took her clutch of eggs,

Carefully, to our own bed?
They hatched out under our heat,
Their first passions being earth
And water, the sky that curved

Far over the huddling barns.
We taught the fields of kept corn
Good for both bread and porridge,
And as they were then of age,

The rightness of wearing clothes.
We hooked up their rubber shoes
For that sad day they waddled
Back into their rightful wild,

The heaven of river banks.
They had learned to speak our tongue,
Knew it was all for the best.
Was that not the year you lost

Another child, the oil slick
Again bloodied our own creek,
All innocents were set free,
Your father had learned to fly?

CUCKOO CORN

The seed that goes into the ground
After the first cuckoo
Is said to grow short and light
As the beard of a boy.

Though Spring was slow this year
And the seed late,
After that Summer the corn was long
And heavy as the hair of any girl.

They claimed that she had no errand
Near the thresher,
This girl whose hair floated as if underwater
In a wind that would have cleaned corn,

Who was strangled by the flapping belt.
But she had reason,
I being her lover, she being that man's daughter,
Knowing of cuckoo corn, of seed and season.

THE FIELD HOSPITAL

Taking, giving back their lives
By the strength of our bare hands,
By the silence of our knives,
We answer to no grey South

Nor blue North, not self defence,
The lie of just wars, neither
Cold nor hot blood's difference
In their discharging of guns,

But that hillside of fresh graves.
Would this girl brought to our tents
From whose flesh we have removed
Shot that George, on his day off,

Will use to weight fishing lines,
Who died screaming for ether,
Yet protest our innocence?
George lit the lanterns, in danced

Those gigantic, yellow moths
That brushed right over her wounds,
Pinning themselves to our sleeves
Like medals given the brave.

MULES

LUNCH WITH PANCHO VILLA

I

'Is it really a revolution, though?'
I reached across the wicker table
With another $10,000 question.
My celebrated pamphleteer,
Co-author of such volumes
As *Blood on the Rose*,
The Dream and the Drums,
And *How It Happened Here*,
Would pour some untroubled Muscatel
And settle back in his cane chair.

'Look, son. Just look around you.
People are getting themselves killed
Left, right and centre
While you do what? Write rondeaux?
There's more to living in this country
Than stars and horses, pigs and trees,
Not that you'd guess it from your poems.
Do you never listen to the news?
You want to get down to something true,
Something a little nearer home.'

*

41

I called again later that afternoon,
A quiet suburban street.
'You want to stand back a little
When the world's at your feet.'
I'd have liked to have heard some more
Of his famous revolution.
I rang the bell, and knocked hard
On what I remembered as his front door,
That opened then, as such doors do,
Directly on to a back yard.

II

Not any back yard, I'm bound to say,
And not a thousand miles away
From here. No one's taken in, I'm sure,
By such a mild invention.
But where (I wonder myself) do I stand,
In relation to a table and chair,
The quince-tree I forgot to mention,
That suburban street, the door, the yard —
All made up as I went along
As things that people live among.

And such a person as lived there!
My celebrated pamphleteer!
Of course, I gave it all away
With those preposterous titles.
The Bloody Rose? The Dream and the Drums?
The three-day-wonder of the flowering plum!
Or was I desperately wishing
To have been their other co-author,
Or, at least, to own a first edition
Of *The Boot Boys and Other Battles?*

'When are you going to tell the truth?'
For there's no such book, so far as I know,
As *How it Happened Here,*
Though there may be. There may.
What should I say to this callow youth
Who learned to write last winter —
One of those correspondence courses —
And who's coming to lunch today?
He'll be rambling on, no doubt,
About pigs and trees, stars and horses.

THE CENTAURS

I can think of William of Orange,
Prince of gasworks-wall and gable-end.
A plodding, snow-white charger
On the green, grassy slopes of the Boyne,
The milk-cart swimming against the current

Of our own backstreet. Hernan Cortes
Is mustering his cavalcade on the pavement,
Lifting his shield like the lid of a garbage-can.
His eyes are fixed on a river of Aztec silver,
He whinnies and paws the earth

For our amazement. And Saul of Tarsus,
The stone he picked up once has grown into a hoof.
He slings the saddle-bags over his haunches,
Lengthening his reins, loosening his girth,
To thunder down the long road to Damascus.

THE BIG HOUSE

I was the only girl under the stairs
But I was the first to notice something was wrong.
I was always first up and about, of course.
Those hens would never lay two days running
In the same place. I would rise early
And try round the haggard for fresh nests.
The mistress let me keep the egg-money.

And that particular night there were guests,
Mrs de Groot from the bridge set
And a young man who wrote stories for children,
So I wanted everything to be just right
When they trooped down to breakfast that morning.

I slept at the very top of that rambling house,
A tiny room with only a sky-light window.
I had brushed my hair and straightened my dress
And was just stepping into the corridor
When it struck me. That old boarded-up door
Was flung open. A pile of rubble and half-bricks
Was strewn across the landing floor.

I went on down. I was stooping among the hay-stacks
When there came a clatter of hooves in the yard.
The squire's sure-footed little piebald mare
Had found her own way home, as always.
He swayed some. Then fell headlong on the cobbles.

*

45

There was not so much as the smell of whiskey on him.
People still hold he had died of fright,
That the house was haunted by an elder brother
Who was murdered for his birthright.
People will always put two and two together.

What I remember most of that particular morning
Was how calmly everyone took the thing.
The mistress insisted that life would go on quietly
As it always had done. Breakfast was served
At nine exactly. I can still hear Mrs de Groot
Telling how she had once bid seven hearts.
The young man's stories were for grown-ups, really.

EPONA

I have no heart, she cries. I am driving her madder,
Out of her depth, almost, in the tall grass
Of Parsons' triangular meadow.
Because I straddle some old jackass

Whose every hoof curves like the blade
Of a scythe. It staggers over
Towards a whitethorn hedge, meaning to rid
Itself of me. Just in time I slither

Off the sagging, flabbergasted back.
To calm a jackass, they say, you take its ear like a snaffle
Between your teeth. I bite her ear and shoo her back
Into the middle of my life.

CASS AND ME

Do you remember me, Cass,
The brim of his hat over my face,
My father's slicker trailing the ground
When I was a child? Once you came round

And I climbed on your shoulders.
Once you were stronger, taller, older.
We leaned out across the yard
As a giant would across the world.

The sow fled West with her farrow,
The hound made a rainbow under the barrow.
The cock crowed out of time,

So large we loomed.
Which of us, I wonder, had grown,
Whose were those wide eyes at my groin?

HOW TO PLAY CHAMPIONSHIP TENNIS

That winter of my third-form year,
While the other boys played penny poker
Or listened to the latest Hendrix,
Or simply taunted Joe and Cyril,

I fell in with the school caretaker.
He was like me, from the country,
We seemed to speak the same language.
He knew the names of all the trees,

He knew them by their wizened leaves.
Books, too. He had gathered hundreds.
He loved their very smells, their shapes.
There was this book that I might like

That he would give me as a present.
How to Play Championship Tennis.
We would meet the next morning at break
In his little workshop.

The book lay squarely on the table.
I reached for it. But as I stooped
He leaned across and grabbed my pecker.
I ran out by the unkempt lawn

Through a fine, insinuating drizzle.
The net had long been taken down
Yet here were Joe and Cyril, knocking up;
Their fluent lobs, their deft volleys,

As if they had found some other level.

49

CHEESECAKE

The mother was going through
An old chest of drawers
When she found the plain brown envelope
Among his childhood things.
The name she had given her son
Was never this name in such ugly type.
When she opened the envelope
There was a sheaf
Of photographs in cellophane.
Should he not somehow
Have been the one confused,
Did she not even now hold the proof?
When, all of a sudden, there,
And there once more,
Among those bodies her own body posed.

NED SKINNER

Was 'a barbaric yawp',
If you took Aunt Sarah at her word.
He would step over the mountain
Of a summer afternoon
To dress a litter of pigs
On my uncle's farm.

Aunt Sarah would keep me in,
Taking me on her lap
Till it was over.
Ned Skinner wiped his knife
And rinsed his hands
In the barrel at the door-step.

He winked, and gripped my arm.
'It doesn't hurt, not so's you'd notice,
And God never slams one door
But another's lying open.
Them same pigs can see the wind.'
My uncle had given him five shillings.

Ned Skinner came back
While my uncle was in the fields.
'Sarah,' he was calling, 'Sarah.
You weren't so shy in our young day.
You remember yon time in Archer's loft?'
His face blazed at the scullery window.
'Remember? When the hay was won.'

*

Aunt Sarah had the door on the snib.
'That's no kind of talk
To be coming over. Now go you home.'
Silence. Then a wheeze.
We heard the whiskey-jug
Tinkle, his boots diminish in the yard.
Aunt Sarah put on a fresh apron.

MA

Old photographs would have her bookish, sitting
Under a willow. I take that to be a croquet
Lawn. She reads aloud, no doubt from Rupert Brooke.
The month is always May or June.

Or with the stranger on the motor-bike.
Not my father, no. This one's all crew-cut
And polished brass buttons.
An American soldier, perhaps.
                                    And the full moon
Swaying over Keenaghan, the orchards and the cannery,
Thins to a last yellow-hammer, and goes.
The neighbours gather, all Keenaghan and Collegelands,
There is story-telling. Old miners at Coalisland
Going into the ground. Swinging, for fear of the gas,
The soft flame of a canary.

KEEN

after the Irish

I never dreamt you would die
Till your horse came back to me
With long reins trailing,
Your blood on its brow
And your polished saddle

Empty. I started up quickly.
One leap from the settle,
The next to the lintel,
A final fling as far as the stirrup.
I went off at full gallop.

I would find you stretched
By that low whin bush
Without pope or bishop,
Without priest or monk
To preside or pray over you,

But some withered, old woman
Who had wrapped you in her mantle.
Your blood was flowing still,
I knew of no way to staunch it.
I cupped my hands and drank it.

VAQUERO

He has blown in from the badlands
Where, steadily coming to grief

Through hunger and thirst
And his belly too big for his eyes,

He must have lashed himself
Upright in the ornamental saddle

On this dilapidated, riddled
Jennet. He has been dead a week now,

His face blue-green, mulatto.
And the halo of buzzards

That was once a rippling, swirling lasso
No wider now than his hat-band.

OUR LADY OF ARDBOE

I

Just there, in a corner of the whin-field,
Just where the thistles bloom.
She stood there as in Bethlehem
One night in nineteen fifty-three or four.

The girl leaning over the half-door
Saw the cattle kneel, and herself knelt.

II

I suppose that a farmer's youngest daughter
Might, as well as the next, unravel
The winding road to Christ's navel.

Who's to know what's knowable?
Milk from the Virgin Mother's breast,
A feather off the Holy Ghost?
The fairy thorn? The holy well?

Our simple wish for there being more to life
Than a job, a car, a house, a wife —
The fixity of running water.

For I like to think, as I step these acres,
That a holy well is no more shallow
Nor plummetless than the pools of Shiloh,
The fairy thorn no less true than the Cross.

56

III

Mother of our Creator, Mother of our Saviour,
Mother most amiable, Mother most admirable.
Virgin most prudent, Virgin most venerable,
Mother inviolate, Mother undefiled.

And I walk waist-deep among purples and golds
With one arm as long as the other.

BIG LIZ

After the sleekness of moleskin trews
I seem at last to have got to grips
With this old collier.
He hunkers over his pint of bitter

In his best suit and starched collar.
Somehow, this half-hearted stripper
Sheds new light on herself and him.
She opens up before us like a seam,

Stepping back through the hoops
Of flannel petticoats, the grain of trees,
To the inevitability of earth.

And though our cheers might raise the roof
He hunkers still, his hard eye level
With the diamond in her navel.

THE DUCKING STOOL

While they were squatting stark naked
On those hollowed, chalky flags
She had taken no oaths
Nor pow-wowed with twelve devils
Nor worn the collar of a Pater Noster
Front to back or back to front,

Neither whispered the Horseman's Word
Nor kissed the buttocks
Of anything like a yearling goat.
This was nothing if not mild.
He got up all of a sudden and left her
At the bottom of a garden.

                              A child
Sitting out her Sabbaths
The rickety, only child on the see-saw.
Was no one coming back to play,
Might a life not hang in the balance?
No abler then to prove her blamelessness

Than were Maeve and Bronagh,
Rowena and Morag, such sisters
As drowned on that long arm of the law,
Nor ready for such logic.
She was summoned now by her grand-father
For another game of hide-and-seek

*

Through the ancient, three-storey rectory
He knew like the back of his hand.
She would crouch in some narrow wardrobe
Among stinking, mildewed foxes
While his steps faltered at the door,
Which, opening, might throw light on her.

THE GIRLS IN THE POOLROOM

The girls in the poolroom
Were out on their own limbs.

How could I help
But make men of them?

There was Emily
Who was lovely and tall and slim.

I used to meet her in the pub
And sometimes she came home.

She raved about Albert Camus
And the twenty-third psalm.

I asked her once, 'Are you asleep?'
She said, 'I am. I am.'

BOON

'And what's the snow that melts the soonest?'
Mercy was thirteen, maybe fourteen.
'And how would you catch a yellow bittern?'
She was half-way down the mountainside

Before I'd realised. 'I would be right glad
If you knew next Sunday.' Her parting shot
Left me more intent than Lancelot
Upon the Grail. Or whoever it was. Sir Galahad.

'A yellow bittern?' I'd consulted Will Hunter,
Who carried a box of matches
And had gone by himself to the pictures.
He wrinkled his nose. 'I know green linnets

You take with just a pinch of salt
On their tails. That's according to most people.
A yellow bittern. They might be special.'
'And the snow that's first to melt?'

I'd got that wrong. He was almost certain.
'The snow that scarcely ever lies
Falls on a lady's breasts and thighs.'
That week stretched longer than the Creation!

We climbed the hills to the highest hill-farm
Without a word of snow or bittern
And viewed the extravagant wilderness
Of the brawling townlands round the Moy,

The cries from the football-field grown so dim
We might be listening on the wireless.
When I'd all but forgotten that she'd forgotten
Mercy would take me in her arms.

THE WOOD

They tell me how they bought
An hour of silence
From a juke-box in New York
Or San Francisco once,

That now they intend
To go back to their home place
For a bit of peace,

A house overlooking a lake
And a wood for kindling.

'But you can't fell trees
That have stood for as long
As anyone remembers?'

'The wood we have in mind will stand
While it has lost its timber.'

AT MASTER MCGRATH'S GRAVE

I

He had a long white streak
On his deep chest,
A small white patch
Over one of his shoulders,
And two white claws
One each of his forepaws.

Over his lean back
He was all ticked with white,
As if a shower of hail
Had fallen and never melted.

II

Should he not still smoulder,
Our shooting star,
That claimed the Waterloo Cup
In eighteen sixty-nine?

I'm standing at the edge
Of Lord Lurgan's demesne
Where the Master is stretched
Under his plinth,
A bucket of quicklime
Scattered all along his length.

*

III

The overhanging elm-trees
And the knee-high grass
Are freshly tinged
By this last sun-shower.

I'm not beside myself with grief,
Not even so taken by McGrath,

It's just the way these elm-trees
Do more and more impinge,
The knee-high grass
Has brought me to my knees.

BLEMISH

Were it indeed an accident of birth
That she looks on the gentle earth
And the seemingly gentle sky
Through one brown, and one blue eye.

THE BEARDED WOMAN, BY RIBERA

I've seen one in a fairground,
Swigging a quart of whiskey,
But nothing like this lady
Who squats in the foreground
To suckle the baby,
With what must be her husband
Almost out of the picture.

Might this be the Holy Family
Gone wrong?

Her face belongs to my grand-da
Except that her beard
Is so luxuriantly black.
One pap, her right, is bared
And borrowed by her child,
Who could not be less childlike.
He's ninety, too, if he's a day.

I'm taken completely
By this so unlikely Madonna.

Yet my eye is drawn once again,
Almost against its wishes,
To the figure in the shadows,
Willowy, and clean-shaven,
As if he has simply wandered in
Between mending that fuse
And washing the breakfast dishes.

THE MERMAN

He was ploughing his single furrow
Through the green, heavy sward
Of water. I was sowing winter wheat
At the shoreline, when our farms met.

Not a furrow, quite, I argued.
Nothing would come of his long acre
But breaker growing out of breaker,
The wind-scythe, the rain-harrow.

Had he no wish to own such land
As he might plough round in a day?
What of friendship, love? Such qualities?

He remembered these same fields of corn or hay
When swathes ran high along the ground,
Hearing the cries of one in difficulties.

PARIS

A table for two will scarcely seat
The pair of us! All the people we have been
Are here as guests, strategically deployed
As to who will go best with whom.
A convent girl, a crashing bore, the couple

Who aren't quite all they seem.
A last shrimp curls and winces on your plate
Like an embryo. 'Is that a little overdone?'
And these country faces at the window
That were once our own. They study the menu,

Smile faintly, and are gone.
Chicken Marengo! It's a far cry from the Moy.
'There's no such person as Saint Christopher,
Father Talbot gave it out at Mass.
Same as there's no such place as Limbo.'

The world's less simple for being travelled,
Though. In each fresh, neutral place
Where our differences might have been settled
There were men sitting down to talk of peace
Who began with the shape of the table.

THE NARROW ROAD TO THE DEEP NORTH

A Japanese soldier
Has just stumbled out of the forest.
The war has been over
These thirty years, and he has lost

All but his ceremonial sword.
We offer him an American cigarette.
He takes it without a word.
For all this comes too late. Too late

To break the sword across his knee,
To be right or wrong.
He means to go back to his old farm

And till the land. Though never to deny
The stone its sling,
The blade of grass its one good arm.

THE MIXED MARRIAGE

My father was a servant-boy.
When he left school at eight or nine
He took up billhook and loy
To win the ground he would never own.

My mother was the school-mistress,
The world of Castor and Pollux.
There were twins in her own class.
She could never tell which was which.

She had read one volume of Proust,
He knew the cure for farcy.
I flitted between a hole in the hedge
And a room in the Latin Quarter.

When she had cleared the supper-table
She opened *The Acts of the Apostles*,
Aesop's Fables, Gulliver's Travels.
Then my mother went on upstairs

And my father further dimmed the light
To get back to hunting with ferrets
Or the factions of the faction-fights,
The Ribbon Boys, the Caravats.

DE SECRETIS MULIERUM

They're nothing, really, all the girls I've known
With legs up their oxters,
Their hair all blossom and their long bones
Laden with fruit,
Nothing to Harry Conway's daughter.

Don't get me wrong — it's not as if she's awkward.
If you can picture a dappled orchard
That's scarcely been touched by frost,
And where all those other tits and bums
Are deep in conversation. What weight they've lost!
What windfalls strew the pathways!

Well, she's the one, if you can make her out,
Whose head is full — no, not of pears, not plums —
But pomegranates, pawpaws.

LARGESSE

A body would think
The world was its meat and drink.

It fits like a dream!
What's the fish-pond to the fish,
Avocado and avocado-dish,
But things shaped by their names?

For only by embroidery
Will a star take root in the sky,
A flower have a pillow for ground.
How many angels stand on a pinhead?

Twelve o'clock. We climb to bed.
A trout leaps in the far pond,
The sound of one hand clapping.

And the avocado-stone is mapping
Its future through the wreck
Of dinner-table and dining-room.

Numberless cherubim and seraphim
Alleluia on my prick!

CIDER

Though we lie by their sides we may never know
The lengths to which our roads might go,
Or so we like to think. They end as we end —
Dead in their beds, going round the bend,

In mid-sentence at quays.
I have lain by your side for long enough,
Our sheets are littered with those yellow moths
That wanted only their names in lights.

I want you to bring me down to the estuary.
At low tide we might wade out to an island, Hy
Brasil, the Land of Youth.

I'm through with drinking for another night,
Lead me down to the estuary. While I'm in two minds,
Now that the glass had taken my other hand.

THE RUCKSACK

That morning Lars fell
He dragged the rest
Down with him.

My base-camp flickers,
True if small,
Where I buried them.

My eyes have failed,
My beard is blue with rime.
I hack another step

From the perpendicular.
Should I give up, turn back?
When, that one step

Ahead, on the crest,
Stands my little Sherpa,
Wild and weatherbeaten,

Lending me a hand.
He wears my own old rucksack
From the first expedition.

AT MARTHA'S DELI

So Will had finally broken off with Faith!
There she stood, gnawing a shish-kebab.
It seemed they no longer soaked in one bath-tub
And made that kind of little wave.

Now she came over, wiping her hands in her dress
And asking if I might not be her friend.
I led her down through the bracken
And listened again to what the doctors told her

Of how she might live only a year,
To where earlier on I had come upon the vixen
That must have thought this her finest kill.

The taste of blood on a greased knife
Whereby she would happily drink herself to death.
She kissed me hard. I might have been her own Will.

THE COUNTRY CLUB

'But what would interest you about the brook,
It's always cold in summer, warm in winter.'
'Warm in December, cold in June, you say?'
Doc Pinkerton was a great one for chapter and verse.

'I don't suppose the water's changed at all.
You and I know enough to know it's warm
Compared with cold, and cold compared with warm,
But all the fun's in how you say a thing.'

'Well, it shouldn't seem true when it's not.'
He took out his watch. 'I'd best be getting home.'

Just after three. The bar was shutting down.
Ella Stafford was high as a kite.
She was wearing one of those little black dresses
And a kiss-curl something like Veronica Lake's.

She was right side of thirty, husband out of town,
It seemed I might have fallen on my feet.

Neither of them was so far gone, as it turned out.
She slept the whole way to their villa
On the Heights. She kissed me wetly on the chin
And staggered in through the bougainvillaea.

I fetched a pot of coffee from an all-night café
And drove up to watch the new day breaking.

Cicadas were clipping the lawns and ornamental bushes.
I was coming back down onto the highway
When I met Lee Pinkerton's Chevrolet.
We drew up close. He rolled down his window.

'There's been some trouble over Stafford's way.
Took a shot at his wife.' He gave me a knowing look.
'She'd been seeing a lot of some other fella,
Or so it seems. I can't make head nor tail of it.'

BANG

For that moment we had been the others
These things happen to —
A tree would give its neighbour the elbow
And both look the other way,
The birds were whistling
At the ordinariness of it all.
Our slow coming to in a renovated clearing,
The farfetched beginning to reassemble.
Which of us had that leg belonged to?

It brought me back years to that Carnival
In the next parish — the football pitch, the striped marquee
And the dark's unrestricted parking —
The priest who built them on his hands and knees
Beside some girl who had lost an ear-ring,
She moaning the name of the one who scored the goal
Earlier that evening.

DUFFY'S CIRCUS

Once Duffy's Circus had shaken out its tent
In the big field near the Moy
God may as well have left Ireland
And gone up a tree. My father has said so.

There was no such thing as the five-legged calf,
The God of Creation
Was the God of Love.
My father chose to share such Nuts of Wisdom.

Yet across the Alps of each other the elephants
Trooped. Nor did it matter
When Wild Bill's Rain Dance
Fell flat. Some clown emptied a bucket of stars

Over the swankiest part of the crowd.
I had lost my father in the rush and slipped
Out the back. Now I heard
For the first time that long-drawn-out cry.

It came from somewhere beyond the corral.
A dwarf on stilts. Another dwarf.
I sidled past some trucks. From under a freighter
I watched a man sawing a woman in half.

MULES

Should they not have the best of both worlds?

Her feet of clay gave the lie
To the star burned in our mare's brow.
Would Parsons' jackass not rest more assured
That cross wrenched from his shoulders?

We had loosed them into one field.
I watched Sam Parsons and my quick father
Tense for the punch below their belts,
For what was neither one thing or the other.

It was as though they had shuddered
To think, of their gaunt, sexless foal
Dropped tonight in the cowshed.

We might yet claim that it sprang from earth
Were it not for the afterbirth
Trailed like some fine, silk parachute,
That we would know from what heights it fell.

ARMAGEDDON, ARMAGEDDON

I

At last, someone had heard tell of Larry Durrell.
We leaned round headland after headland
When there it was, his Snow-White Villa.
Wasn't it dazzling?
                            Well, it was rather white.
The orange and lemon groves, the olives,
Are wicked for this purity of light.
In a while now we will go ashore, to Mouse Island.

The light is failing. Our mouths are numb with aniseed,
Her little breasts are sour as Jeanne Duval's.
And darknesses weigh down further the burgeoning trees
Where she kneels in her skimpy dress
To gather armful after armful.
Nuzzling the deep blues, the purples. Spitting the stars.

*

II

When Oisin came back to Ireland
After three hundred years
On one of those enchanted islands
Somewhere in the Western Seas,

He thought nothing of dismounting
From his enchanted steed
To be one again with the mountains,
The bogs and the little fields.

There and then he began to stoop,
His hair, and all his teeth, fell out,
A mildewed belt, a rusted buckle.
The clays were heavy, black or yellow,
Those were the colours of his boots.
And I know something of how he felt.

III

Not to worry. From where I lived
We might watch Long Bullets being played,
Follow the course of a pair of whippets,
Try to keep in time with a Lambeg Drum.

There'd be Derryscollop, and Cloveneden,
The parish where W. R. Rodgers held sway.
And where the first Orange Lodge was founded,
An orchard full of No Surrenders.

We could always go closer if you wanted,
To where Macha had challenged the charioteer
And Swift the Houyhnhnm,
The open field where her twins were whelped.
Then, the scene of the Armagh Rail Disaster.
Why not brave the Planetarium?

*

IV

You had been sleeping, o my lover,
A good half-hour, it seemed,
And I woke you only to discover
How you might have dreamed,
How you might have dreamed.

Might some glistening inspector
By his one dull incisor
And simple rule-of-thumb
Already have beavered through
To our last-carriage-but-one?

Did he hint something of blockades,
Of trees felled across the lines,
And then hand back our tickets
Ratified by their constellations?

V

Now that I had some idea of our whereabouts
We could slow a little and not be afraid.
Who was that? Only the bull behind the hedge,
It was showing us the whites of its eyes.

Why should those women be carrying water
If all the wells were poisoned, as they said,
And the fish littering the river?
Had the sheep been divided from the goats,
Were Twin and Twin at each other's throats?

I knew these fields. How long were they fallow?
Those had been Archer's sixty yellow acres,
These Hunter's forty green and grey.
Had Hunter and Archer got it into their heads
That they would take the stars in their strides?

*

VI

My brother had mislaid his voice
Since it happened. His eyes had grown simple,
His hand alone would describe
Our father's return from the betting-shop
To be torn between his own two ponies,
Their going their different ways.

He had guarded our mother bent-double
Over the kitchen sink, her face in the basin.
She had broken another of her best dishes,
We would bury her when we were able.

Some violence had been done to Grace,
She had left for our next-of-kin.
My brother gave us half of his last mangold
And the warning of bayonets fixed in the bushes.

VII

A summer night in Keenaghan
So dark my light had lingered near its lamp
For fear of it. Nor was I less afraid.
At the Mustard Seed Mission all was darkness.

I had gone out with the kettle
To a little stream that lay down in itself
And breathed through a hollow reed
When yon black beetle lighted on my thumb
And tickled along my palm
Like a blood-blister with a mind of its own.

My hand might well have been some flat stone
The way it made for the underside.
I had to turn my wrist against its wont
To have it walk in the paths of uprightness.